BOA
EDITIONS LTD

The Reindeer Camps
and Other Poems

The Reindeer Camps

and Other Poems
by Barton Sutter

American Poets Continuum Series, No. 133

BOA Editions, Ltd. ❖ Rochester, NY ❖ 2012

8/12

First Edition
12 13 14 15   7 6 5 4 3 2 1

For information about permission to reuse any material from this book please contact The
Permissions Company at www.permissionscompany.com or e-mail permdude@eclipse.net.

Publications by BOA Editions, Ltd.—a not-for-profit corporation
under section 501 (c) (3) of the United States Internal Revenue
Code—are made possible with funds from a variety of sources, in-
cluding public funds from the New York State Council on the Arts,
a state agency; the Literature Program of the National Endowment
for the Arts; the County of Monroe, NY; the Lannan Foundation for
support of the Lannan Translations Selection Series; the Mary S. Mul-
ligan Charitable Trust; the Rochester Area Community Foundation;
the Arts & Cultural Council for Greater Rochester; the Steeple-Jack
Fund; the Ames-Amzalak Memorial Trust in memory of Henry Ames, Semon Amzalak and
Dan Amzalak; and contributions from many individuals nationwide. See Colophon on page
128 for special individual acknowledgments.

ART WORKS.
arts.gov

State of the Arts

NYSCA

Cover Design: Daphne Morrissey
Cover Photograph: Dexter Thue
Interior Design and Composition: Richard Foerster
Manufacturing: Thomson-Shore
BOA Logo: Mirko

Library of Congress Cataloging-in-Publication Data

Sutter, Barton, 1949–
 The reindeer camps and other poems / by Barton Sutter. — 1st ed.
    p. cm.
 ISBN 978-1-934414-84-2 (pbk. : alk. paper)
 I. Title.
 PS3569.U87R45 2012
 811'.54—dc23

                              2011036859

BOA Editions, Ltd.
250 North Goodman Street, Suite 306
Rochester, NY 14607
www.boaeditions.org
A. Poulin, Jr., Founder (1938–1996)

For
Philip Dacey

Contents

I

Alakazam

In therapy for swilling
Booze and women both,
I wrote my way back home
To that dangerous green room
Where my young mother,
Breastless, bald, and blind,
Shrieked and called and screamed
While the candy-striped hi-fi
Spun music sickly sweet
By Wayne King and His Orchestra:
"You'd Be So Nice to Come Home To,"
"The Way You Look Tonight."

And suddenly I understood
My inability to waltz
And how I clamped my hands
Like earmuffs to my head
And stumbled from the house
To runrun, runaway,
Shouting as I ran: "Just
Go ahead and die, then.
Die!"

Nestlings

The blue smoke stank, the chainsaws snarled,
The popples thrashed and thumped the ground.
Of all my memories of that world,
Why should this keep coming round?

I stood way back—excited, sad—
As light exploded through the shade.
The swarming men all knew my dad,
Which made me somewhat less afraid.

But then big Nils called out to me,
And I walked over, hesitant,
Where he had limbed a fallen tree.
"Look," he said, and crooked a hand.

The wood gave off a pungent scent.
Sawdust powdered Nils' wrists.
Hands on knees, I slowly bent
To see where he said, "Look at this."

The pale green trunk, smooth as skin,
Was punctured by a perfect hole;
Woodpecker nestlings peeped within,
Featherless and vulnerable.

I smiled at Nils. He grinned at me
And placed a huge hand on my head.
"We'll tie this to another tree
So the parent birds come back," he said.

I don't remember that they did.
Undoubtedly, those nestlings died.
The frightened parents must have fled,
But I like thinking how Nils tried.

That site where our new house was built
Got cleared of scrapwood in one day,
But I was touched by fear and guilt,
A shadow that would stay.

What Does This Mean?

In those days, eighth-grade boys drove cars,
Grain trucks, and tractors on the farm,
So Dad was only half-surprised
The little men he catechized
Drove themselves to the village school
(Cream and milk, not church and state,
Were what they worked to separate)
Where he recounted Luther's rules.

Thou shalt have no other gods before me.
What does this mean?

We lived so near to Canada
No one was shocked that Saturday a
Black bear loomed outside the glass
Where Dad was questioning his class.
The kids evacuated, rushed
To pickup trucks and beater Fords
To chase the bear down gravel roads
But lost him in the underbrush.

Thou shalt not covet thy neighbor's wife,
Nor his manservant, nor his maidservant,
Nor his ox, nor his ass,
Nor anything that is thy neighbor's.
What does this mean?

My father's teaching was homespun:
Father, Holy Ghost, and Son
Were peanuts in a single shell.
His ways were easy, slow, soft-sell.
To those who could not memorize,

He'd feed the answers, phrase by phrase.
Some girls would stammer in his gaze,
Distracted by his light blue eyes.

Thou shalt not commit adultery.
What does this mean?

They'd work an hour, then take a break
For thirty minutes the boys would make
The most of, charging through our woods,
Chasing rabbits, hot for blood,
Armed with pebbles and slingshots,
Helter-skelter, crashing brush,
With shouts and yelps when one would flush,
And then return to talk of God.

Thou shalt not kill.
What does this mean?

Less than a dozen years before,
My father had come back from war,
Where many of his friends had died.
These churches in the countryside
Called him to marry, bury, bless,
Ambitionless for wealth or fame.
Those few who still recall his name
Remember best his gentleness.

Honor thy father and thy mother
That thy days may be long upon the land.
What does this mean?

The Plaster

How often, here in middle age,
In my comfy house, my kids well clothed,
I'm suddenly back with the Stuberbiers,
Our neighbors in my early years.
Darrel and Dale, jackrabbit boys
Bound to their father's failing farm,
Lived a mile up the asphalt road
From our blinding, pure white parsonage.
Their father drank. Their mother had run.
Did an older sister care for them?

Why was I drawn to the Stuberbiers' ruin,
That poor place weathered gray as rain?
On my first visit, I was floored
To find their dad had pulled the doors
Right off the house for the warmer months.
This meant mosquitoes, flies, and moths
Were unimpeded as the breeze.

A five-year-old doesn't judge but sees.
Except for a feedstore calendar,
The walls of this blank house were bare.
In my friends' bedroom, my small heart froze
To see their midden heap of clothes
And understand with dumb distress
That they slept on a raw mattress.

We shouted, ran from room to room,
Our laughter shattering the gloom,
Slathered Kleenex bread with butter,
Covered that with loads of sugar.
Outside, we dropped to knees and hands

To squeeze into the cramped crawlspace—
A filthy, fine, and private place—
To gobble down our contraband
And drug ourselves from the sugar bowl,
Propped on elbows, hares in a hole.

One day, their dad, a man I feared,
Asked us along to his hay pasture.
I shied from such a famous sinner,
Though I adored his Fordson tractor,
And here was a chance to ride the rack,
Jouncing along in the open air.

Out the yard, up the road, back
In the woods to the boggy field.
The hayrack had a bockety wheel,
So we clung to the boards, avoiding slivers.
All around us, popples shivered.
The cut grass lay in thin windrows.
The father let the tractor idle,
Served up the hay in scratchy forkfuls,
While we three eyed those spooky tines
Glinting in the hot sunshine.

The work was a game, however warm.
We swept the hay up in our arms,
Heaped it high, both front and back,
Then tramped the grass till it was packed.
We circled round the scraggly field
Until one heavy tractor wheel
Crushed a hidden hornets' nest.
Darrel was unluckiest.
Drilled above his right eyebrow,
He held his head, hopped, and howled.

As if his screams weren't loud enough,
The father shut the tractor off
And hurried back to check the boy
Who ripped the silence with his noise.
He put one arm around his kid,
Traced the place where he'd been bit,
Clumsily wiping his son's wet face,
Murmuring strange nonsense, too,
That sounded like "Sue, sue, sue, sue."

That bad man then abandoned us,
Stumbling off across the field,
As if this trouble were unreal.
But no, he stooped down in the ditch,
Then hustled back, his arms outstretched,
His oozing, muddy hands gray-blue.
What on earth did he mean to do?

Fifty years have shown me how
A gentleness can sometimes linger:
I see his trembling, farm-thick fingers
Plastering his young son's brow
With a dripping lump of cool blue clay
To take the hornet's sting away.

And then, since we still had grass to stack,
He boosted us back on the bum hayrack.

My Father and the Trondheims

When I was six, I fell in love
With Jean Trondheim, who had a cloud
Of dark brown hair, a happy face, and so
I asked her if she'd marry me,
And she said, "Yes, of course." We kissed
Out in the spruce grove during recess,
So everybody knew that we were married,
Though later, naturally, everyone forgot,
Except (fast forward) in our twenties,
In the city, Jean and I collided
Quite delightfully, and we were
Still in love a little, so we kissed
And went to bed a time or two, but,
You know how it goes, it wasn't meant to be—
Astrological, she said—yet every now and then
She'll surface once again. We always kiss,
And, even though we married other people,
We both know who we married first.
Forever is forever, after all, but memory,
Not marriage, is the subject of this story.

The point is that her little brother drowned.
The Trondheims owned a gravel pit
Outside the tiny town where we grew up,
And that rambunctious family loved
To splash and porpoise in the pit. Who wouldn't?
They had scads of kids, the Trondheims
Being Catholic in those days of meatless Fridays,
Autocratic priests, and guesswork birth control.
The siblings scrapped and helped each other out,
But someone somehow wasn't watching or forgot
Because that day the little brother drank

And drank pit water and went down.
I can't recall the details or the little brother's name,
Except he drowned. And who knows why,
But the priest couldn't come from town somehow,
And so my father, a minister who worried
He'd offend the Trondheims, decided, still,
He'd better go and went. He took his Bible,
This I know, but who knows what he said?
He wasn't very eloquent, I'll bet,
But he was kind, I'm sure. I'm sure
He told them he was sorry, led them in a prayer,
Even as they gagged and gasped for air.

Decades later, anytime that Jean and I
Surprise each other on the street, I see
She's glad to see me, sure, but still I know
She's thinking of that little brother in the water,
For, unfailingly, she will remind me
Of this kindness that my father did the Trondheims long ago,
As if she feared that somehow I'd forgot.
My dad is dead. But not to them, he's not.

The Horse-drawn School Bus

One day, out scouting Miller's Hill,
Playing cowboys, as boys will,
We spied, below the farmer's dump,
Something that made us yelp and jump:
A little house lay on its side.
We cut some poles, then pushed and pried
The building over, back upright,
To see—we shouted our delight—
A horse-drawn school bus! It was ours.
Although it lacked the horse, of course,
Was missing parts and ugly orange,
We'd found our own home on the range,
A place where we could dodge the rain
Or rest after the stress and strain
Of trying to herd Black Angus cattle,
Who always seemed to drift and scatter
Or thunder after us instead,
Unafraid of cap gun kids.

We snacked on apples, PBJs,
Whatever our moms had packed that day,
Which our imaginations smoked
To venison and antelope,
And talked about those missing pupils
Who once had ridden slow to school,
Sitting on these wooden benches,
Looking out these blank windows—
Dead by now, or aging widows,
Someone's trembling grandparents.
We heard the horses' clip-and-clop . . .

Then someone joked to stop such thoughts,
And back to boyhood we returned—
Greenhorns, we knew, with lots to learn.

The Snowlady

A woman came out of the blizzard.
  She pounded on our back door.
She lived by the bend in the river,
  Halfway down to the store.

She collapsed on a chair in the kitchen.
  She'd come to my parents for help.
She was running away from her husband,
  Who had beaten her with a belt.

Would my dad please drive her to Jackson?
  Could they make it through the snow?
But first, if he'd take her back home,
  She wanted to pick up some clothes.

The Snowlady insisted
  There was nothing to worry about.
"He's drunk," she said. "When I left him,
  He was passed out on the couch."

My father warmed up the wagon.
  My mother tried to say no,
But my dad said it would be okay.
  What luck! I got to go!

We maneuvered into their driveway.
  The woman ran for the house.
I could feel my father's worry
  Till she came hurrying out,

Threw her suitcase in beside me,
    And then jumped in up front.
"Go, go!" she said to my father.
    "He's getting out his gun."

I felt the buzz of adrenaline,
    Though I couldn't have named that thrill.
I was glad we were out of the driveway
    And pulling away uphill.

It was seven miles to Jackson
    And drifting all the way.
The station wagon was floating;
    I could feel it slip and sway.

We found her daughter's apartment.
    The stairs kept climbing higher.
What shocked me, though, I remember,
    Was the bare bulb on its wire.

When the woman unlocked the apartment,
    I stood in the door and stared.
The Snowlady, God help her,
    Seemed delighted to be there.

We drove back into the blizzard.
    I was quiet, contemplative,
Absorbing my new education
    In the ways that people live.

The Pit

The abandoned pit was our Wild West,
   Where we galloped on foot and then
Lit up our stolen cigarettes,
   Midget Marlboro men.

This Western landscape came complete
   With an aspen grove and ponds.
The willows grew where we soaked our feet
   And dozed in soft green fronds.

There were buttes and canyons in this world
   The gravel men had left,
Where we watched the swallows sail and swirl.
   They nested in the cliffs.

We dared to stare in badger holes,
   To sample the abyss,
Preparing for our grown-up roles,
   For deeper darknesses.

Of all our days at the gravel pit,
   There's one that haunts me most,
When each boy clambered up a butte
   To strip off all his clothes.

These pedestals weren't far apart;
   We could shout to one another.
But I felt alone with my thudding heart,
   Like Isaac on his altar.

The breeze blew softly over me;
   The light was woman-warm.
I was cradled by some mystery
   And watched myself grow hard.

I've never truly understood:
   Was it sex? Was it religion?
Each boy lay bare on a grassy butte,
   Defenseless under heaven.

What I Saw in Smitty's Garage

Of course I'd often witnessed nursing kids,
    And any mother's newborn stirred the hope
    That I might watch it snuffle, suck, and grope.
I knew I'd never see a lady naked,
But then at Smitty's place I sort of did.
    I looked into a tiny telescope
    And felt a jolt, as if I'd taken dope,
To spy a blonde, her breasts exhibited.
Smitty had a shoebox spilling with them!
    I couldn't breathe. I trembled, couldn't speak,
Felt guilty, sure, but also born again
    For adoration, kiss and suck and tweak,
And prayed someday I'd find a loving woman
    Who'd let me gaze my fill instead of peek.

The Rubber Breast

Everyone had heard about my mother's cancer.
At Smitty's, someone said, "They took her breast."
Defending her, I heard my heated answer:
"As if some creep like you had seen my mom undressed."
They cut their gossip then, gave it a rest.

Next day—the sight was utterly entrancing—
I saw, clipped to the line where clothes were dancing,
My mother's dripping artificial breast.

A Mighty Fortress

The day was cold and snowy
  They eased her in the ground
In a copper-colored casket, bright
  As pennies I had found.

I couldn't watch my brother
  Or touch my younger sis.
Somehow the little buggers
  Would have to live with this.

How odd to see my father
  At a funeral without robes.
The man looked sick. He deserved to be
  For the lies that he had told.

We sang the heavy line he chose
  For carving on her stone:
"A mighty fortress is our God!"
  What crap. We stood alone.

I smiled at the plastic grass
  Someone had laid out—
Like any dumbass couldn't guess
  What hid there like a shout.

But then I glimpsed the frozen clay
  And had to squinch my eyes,
Recalling how my folks had loved
  To lean and harmonize.

"Have thine own way, Lord.
Have thine own way.
Thou are the potter;
I am the clay.
Mold me and make me
After thy will.
Here I am, waiting,
Yielded and still."

We drove away through falling snow.
  I heard the tires hiss—
The Serpent . . . or the vicious god
  Responsible for this.

My Mother at Swan Lake

This is the day which the Lord has made;
let us rejoice and be glad in it.
—Psalms 118:24

A maniac for picnicking,
   She'd pack us up to go
The very first thing in the spring;
   Sometimes we sat in snow!

But we were well into the year;
   The swans had all long gone.
We'd shed, like leaves, our nagging fears.
   The lake went pink and calm.

Her hair'd come back; her light, low laugh;
   Her cancer in "remission,"
A state that gave us some relief
   From pain and vain religion.

My dad had let me start the fire.
   I saw my mom was proud
Of how the flames kept growing higher;
   They wouldn't flicker out.

I've clutched this day near fifty years
   But always felt so stupid
That it could bring the sting of tears
   When there was nothing to it:

My sister makes a small bouquet
   Of weeds and faded asters,
But I can't hear my mother say
   What she bends low to ask her.

My brother's down beside the shore;
   I see his silhouette.
My father calls out, as before,
   "Now don't go getting wet!"

My mother leans against a tree.
   She sighs. I hear her say
Across the half a century,
   "It's been a lovely day."

How to Say North

Nothing says north like a white pine
Unless it's a maple gone red to maroon
Except for the way cedars lean from the shoreline
Nothing says north like a white pine
But birches so bright that they shout about sunshine
And then there's the tamarack's gold in the gloom
But nothing says north like a white pine
Unless it's a maple gone red to maroon

Dead Evergreens

These trees along the shoreline,
  Veiled in pale green gauze,
Remind me of old women
  Who simply won't be bossed

To lie down in the nursing home
  Or quit their cigarettes.
They stay up late with paperbacks
  And seldom call their kids.

Their kids can argue till they're hoarse
  And purple in the face.
They never cared that much for town.
  They've sunk roots in this place.

And here's that bearded hermit,
  Who let his hair go wild,
Whose clothes hung loose as birch bark,
  Though he flashed a gentle smile.

He came to town four times a year
  To meet his few desires.
He did his own damn dentistry
  With whiskey and a pliers.

They say he lived on venison,
  Pickled fish, and berries,
That birds would flutter to his hand,
  Though children thought him scary.

This hunched and twisted cedar
   Looks like a man I knew
Who had to crawl from room to room.
   His dog was crippled, too.

He stuck like lichen to his farm
   And milked a dozen cows
Till a corporate decision
   Finally shut him down.

He'd fry a pan of pork chops
   And cut big chunks of cake.
"Eat up!" he'd shout. "There's one thing
   That nobody can take."

These trees are clearly done for,
   Bound to drop and drown,
But, silver-gray and sturdy still,
   They somehow hold their ground.

I've cut them, feeling desperate,
   Shivering for heat.
Their limbs flashed incandescent.
   Their scent was smoky sweet.

Several Dozen Shades of Green

Down here in the ravine, we have the model
By means of which the sad United Nations
Might actually succeed: Every species
Flies its own peculiar flag—
Raggedy valerian, broadleaf maple, pom-pom of the pine,
The ferns unfurled, tassels of the grass,
And the willow drags its drooping pennants in the water.
Each declares, defiantly, its own identity,
All compete for space and spread and height,
And yet they've all agreed somehow
To work together for the greater good of green.
And aren't we lucky things turned out this way?
What if leaves had been taxicab yellow or, worse yet, dull as mud?
Think how jumpy we'd have been or seriously depressed!
Instead we are soothed and encouraged by green, made semi-serene,
At least for a season, though those of us who walk here in
      December know
This great glorification of chlorophyll, these snowflakes formed of
      cellulose,
This crisscross reach and rush of vegetation is just a passing dream.

The Minnesota Department of Transportation Plans to Straighten Out Highway 1

Was the Department of Transportation
Created to break our starved hearts?
So it would seem. They bulldoze dreams.
Once, where we blasted across a high bridge
And glimpsed, through a lattice of steel,
The flash of the black-and-blue river,
A raft of bluebills aswim in a swirl,
The thrashing white rapids below,
Our looks now boomerang off a blank wall,
The highway turned hallway, one more
Aesthetic atrocity committed, one more
Beauty spot blotted out.

And now they intend to tame Highway 1,
That sweet prime number, that first and best
Rambunctious trunk through the trees,
That primitive, asphalt snake in the woods,
That whoop-de-do carnival ride of a road.
Oh, say it ain't so! Oh, no, no, no.
Didn't these planners have fathers at all
To tell them the journey itself is the goal?
Were their poor mothers so hooked on speed
They could only whisper, "Efficiency!"?
Oh, say it ain't so. Oh, no.

Will we allow them to level the lift
And fall, the swoop and drop,
The rockabye-baby ocean motion
Singing through our spinning wheels,
The lilt of the lullaby lay of the land?
No, no. No more tilt-a-whirl, watch out,

Hit the gas, touch the brake, wake up,
Hug the curve, sliding, gliding, off on a bowbend,
Double back, hairpin, stop-and-go waltz?
Will all this be lost? To what end, pray tell.
To arrive more quickly at a gravel pit
Or the big blue nothing of Lake Superior?

Whoa, Nelly. Don't tell me
We should speed past trees that took
Two hundred years and more to be
The colossal candelabras they've finally become.
Says who? Should MNDOT reduce
Our chance to flush a flustered grouse,
Waken a wolf, startle a deer, frighten a fox,
Or collide with the sudden broad side of a moose?

Save us, preserve us from Euclid's dream,
The gleam in the architect's eye. Leave us
This road like a river's meander through popple and pine.
Let planners surrender their pens, resign.

Those Finnish Folk

for Jim Johnson

Live out to Toivola, skinny woods and bog,
Sorry sort of country, overlooked by most,
Pioneered by people awful fond of failure.
They branch out to Twig, you know, down as far as Esko,
Askov, Bruno, over there to Togo, Effie, Emily,
Tenstrike, Shooks. Wherever you would never,
There you'll find a Finn.

They believe in Sauna, Nudity, and Coffee.
Their wallpaper is birch bark; their La-Z-Boy's a stump.
The women are good-lookers, the menfolk
Not so much. They specialize in blueberries,
Hayfields and alders, rocks and pickled pike.
They don't go in for paint much, like a weathered look:
Tarpaper buildings, wood piled high . . .
Go and introduce yourself. Coffee's always hot.

Their names are Nordic music, silly and profound,
Descended from the polska, calling to the cows,
Whittled willow whistles, woodwinds, drums.
Names like Ada Aho, Paavo Havumaki,
Sulo Saari, Joki Koveroja.
Where'd they learn such laughter? Poverty and wolves.
Love cries of women. Crooning of the loons.
Watching how the crops grow. Here comes the hail.
Water makes a big splash; then it runs away.
Wind whacks the window, sifts through snow.

A Sad How-do-you-do

It's a sad how-do-you-do when a fervent fisherman can't see to tie on his hook. He's fifty-something, and it's already dusk, but the walleyes are biting, and he'd like to fill out. Just one more fish. But he's popped the 6-lb. test on a snag. He swears, pinches a small gold hook from the little plastic box he carries in the breast pocket of his life vest, rests the hook on one knee, snaps the box shut, and returns it to his pocket. Because he's nearsighted and he's going to be doing close work, he props his glasses on top of his head, as if giving his gray hair a chance to view the gray sky more clearly. He tweezers the hook off his right knee with his right thumb and forefinger and transfers it to the light vise-grips formed by his left thumb and forefinger, holding the end with the barbed hook so that the small gold shaft and eye protrude. Now he pinches the thin, nearly transparent monofilament line between his right thumb and forefinger. The sad how-do-you-do has arrived, though he doesn't know that yet. He just thinks he's going to tie on his hook. It's far easier than threading a needle. He's done it a thousand times.

Mink

The mink is a slinky, sly critter
   But quick as a fart when he wants
To dash through his crosshatched habitat
   Of riverine forest and swamp

To straighten a snake from its wiggle,
   Nab a rabbit who's strayed from its house
And bite at the neck until dead,
   Or crunch a warm mouthful of mouse.

He rejects the gossip of red squirrels
   And steers clear of otters, the clowns.
This overgrown weasel's a loner
   Who'll mate but won't hang around.

Except for some white at the collar,
   His coat is dark chocolate brown.
He moves like a shadow in shadows
   And loves to play lost and found.

Camped once on a hump of black gabbro,
   My brother and I caught five pike
And piled their entrails nearby,
   Thinking gulls would clean up the site.

But a mink emerged from the fractures
   That shattered that long point of rock,
Made an undulant run for the gutpile,
   And then we heard mink happytalk.

He dragged the remains of each northern
　　To his cleft in the rocks down below,
Which magnified growls, urgent slurping,
　　And chuckles I'd translate like so:

Oh, chewy, salt goo of intestine!
　　Oh, tender fish liver and heart!
Oh, succulent, sweet juice of eyeball!
　　Oh, which is my favorite part?

So, wealthy women of fashion
　　And overpaid athletes, take note
Of the greedy-guts eater you've chosen
　　To serve as your totem and robe.

River Otter Rag

Sweetwater seal,
Hide-and-go-seeker,
Slippery slider,
Smooth water glider,
You bob and go under,
Awakening wonder.

How can you swim
So far, so long
Where light grows dim
And there's no oxygen?
Did you learn this trick when you were young,
Or were you born with an extra lung?

Were you once a badger
But such a mud lover
That, thrashing through bushes,
You slid among rushes,
Dissolving in water
To surface as otter?

Hissyfit spitter,
Sneezer and wheezer,
Snuffling blowhard,
Why is your chatter
And spluttering blather
So humanly pleasing?

Cruncher of crayfish,
Ingester of insects,
Robber of birds' nests,
You swallow the walleye,
Smelting the bones
In your Bessemer belly.

Ice and snow skidder,
Prankster and kidder,
You dolphin the river
With siblings in summer,
Your brash bravura a
Buoyant brouhaha.

Does play have a purpose?
Amphibious porpoise,
What is your lesson?
That families are fun
And it's ducky to dive?
That we're plumb lucky to be alive?

Unsinkable soap,
Peekaboo periscope,
Curious creature,
Exemplary teacher,
What is it you see
When you gawk back at me?

A Little Shiver

After the news, the forecaster crowed
With excitement about his bad tidings:
Eighteen inches of snow! Take cover!
A little shiver ran through the community.
Children abandoned their homework.
Who cared about the hypotenuse now?
The snowplow driver laid out his long johns.
The old couple, who'd barked at each other
At supper, smiled shyly, turned off the TV,
And climbed the stairs to their queen-size bed
Heaped high with blankets and quilts.
And the aging husky they failed to hear
Scratch the back door, turned around twice
In the yard, settled herself in the snow,
And covered her nose with her tail.

Lessons I Learned from Our Dog Sophie, a Husky-Shepherd Cross My Wife Picked from the Pound Because Sophie Was Pretty and the Only Quiet Dog in the Room, Who Had Been Found Half-Starved, Wandering a Golf Course, Who Ran Away Whenever She Got the Chance, But Still Chose to Live with Us for Thirteen Years

Be like me, the color of ploughed earth and autumn grass;
You'll blend in when you want, win compliments besides.
Cock your head to the ground now and then. Wonder what's down
    there. Dig.
Keep a wet nose and a whiff of the wolf about you. Never forget
The great gift of four legs. Run. Run whenever you can.
Pity the two-legged ones, though they loom above you and dream
    they're in charge.
One of the joys of this life is scouting ahead and ranging around,
But keep checking back on the less adventurous laggards
And look on them with compassion before you dash off.
Whenever you come to a fork in the path, wait for a sign
From the talking heads, for they are less carefree; they have ideas.
Crouch and sleek yourself before unfamiliar peers;
Lay back your ears, narrow your eyes, lower your tail, and growl.
When biting your friends, go easy, go easy.
Know you can run the entire day away
And still be barely rebuked as long as you're back by sundown.
Prodding by snout often results in petting by hand.
After you poop, kick up your heels. Never spend all of your piss in
    one place.
Birds can be snatched out of bushes more often than squirrels can
    be caught on the run.
The earth is worth listening to every once in a while.
There's something down there. Dig. Keep digging.
Welcome new snow not with dread but with bounding abandon.

Rain is something else again. And hail? Hail is hell.

There is little to fear in this world except bridges, firecrackers, and
thunder.

All of these fears can be overcome . . . except firecrackers and
thunder.

A closet, a table, even a grand piano will serve as a den in a pinch.

Yapping's for puppies. Barking's barbaric. Howling,

However, is you, and clears the fog from your lungs.

Howl for your missing master, howl for your missing mistress,

Howl for the children grown up and gone,

Howl for the days they've kept you corralled, howl for the loss

Of your ancestors, no more nights running the frozen rivers by
moonlight,

Howl for every indignity ever visited upon the race of dog,

Howl for the mute frustration of snuffles and woofs,

For the lack of language except for this heartfelt, gutfelt moan

By means of which you make your ultimate loneliness known.

Whining works wonders, but don't overdo it. Butt-sniffing is fun.

Never walk when you can run. Keep digging. Keep digging.

An Afterlife After All

After our dog survived to fifteen or a hundred and five,
After she'd shrugged out of every harness and collar we could
    devise,
After we'd fenced her and yet she ran but always returned, laughing,
    teaching us dogs could laugh,
After hauling small children on sleds and yanking her leash till she
    coughed,
After tearing the stuffing from Stumpy and Stocky and other
    stuffed toys,
After the fetching of sticks, which she kept to herself,
After wearing the chinchilla's cage, including chinchilla, like an
    outsized, hysterical hat,
After stashing strange gifts of dry bread in our neatly made beds,
After the kidnap, driven two hundred miles by people
    convinced that she was their dead pet come back,
After the rescue and her triumphant return,
After teaching us "walk" was a dangerous word that could whip her
    into a whining canine whirligig,
After thousands of rambles along Chester Creek,
    with sniffing, bushwhacking, and belly-deep wading of pools
    for the cool and the lapping of sweet, wild water,
After her muzzle went white and she gradually slowed,
She lost a tooth, and we sat beside her for hours, watching her bleed
    and drool.

After my wife brought her home from the vet, eyes wet,
Having heard the man say "mandibular cancer" and "moving fast,"
We kept her three days, and after she stood at her dish and just
    looked at us,
We knew what we had to do. We dug out her grave
By shovel and pick and by hand, inching through rocks, roots, and
    clay

And walked her three times that last day
And, brushing and brushing, burnished her fur till she shone,
And she received compliments on her looks on the very last day of
    her life.

After boosting her into the back of the car,
After waiting long minutes inside a bare room,
After she sank to the floor and cooled her belly on tile,
The veterinarian entered and stood with his arms at his sides
And kept saying "mercy" like some sort of priest,
And after the laying of hands on her body,
She winced as the needle entered, then slowly relaxed
And lowered her eyelids and lowered her head,
And once her great heart could no longer be heard,
We loaded her into the back of the car and drove home.

After we carried her heavily to the hole,
After we laid a white sheet smooth in the red clay pit,
After uncinching her collar with jingling tags,
After we draped her warm, slack body into the grave,
Her blonde and mahogany fur fit for a Viking queen,
After we placed sweet basswood blooms at her throat,
Then shut her from sight for good with the sheet,
After we raked the dirt over her crumbly and smooth,
And, after some days, found a heart-shaped rock for her headstone
And planted hostas to cover the naked place where she lay,
I finally went for a walk, free of this creature at last.

Free to wander wherever, however long I might wish,
I wished to walk once more the green ravine she had loved,
Free of dog duty at last, no longer trailing that mutt,
But found, as she'd beat me around every bend,
Then returned to check on my progress, that she was already there,
Everywhere, after preceding me into the Valley of Death,

Gazing back for a moment from every bend in the path,
As if to say, "Are you coming?"

After years of disbelieving in heaven
And laughing off any Valhalla for pets,
I saw that, after all, there was this afterlife at least,
Our living, diminishing memories of the dead,
And I said, through my disbelief and the fog of my grief,
To the ghost of this very old girl in my head,
"Good dog, dead dog, good dog."

III

The Love Song of Karl C. Rove

The first time I laid eyes on him, my God,
I knew I'd found the perfect man for me.
Instead of feeling shamed or slightly odd,
I was, near him, the man I'd meant to be.
He had the cocky swagger that says money.
He crackled with charisma. And that grin!
The down-home, easy manner? He was funny!
I knew right then that I would have to have him.
His Levis were so tight I read the brand
Of snuffbox stuffed inside his pants. I'd wait
For him. I trembled, reached out, took his hand,
And it was firm. The man was absolutely great
With nicknames, but not everybody got 'em,
So I felt blessed he called me his Turd-Blossom.

Laura: Love Song with Accidentals

I don't like to talk about the accident.
   Old news. It happened half a million years ago;
   And George, from Midland, too, of course, was in the know
About the sorry facts: how I was negligent,
A dreamy kid responsible for violence.
   Preoccupied, I smoked and yakked and failed to slow
   Or even see the stop sign flare. Oh, God. And so
I smashed a Corvair broadside, killed its occupant,
   A well-liked boy I liked myself, had tried to date.
I've felt half numb with wonderment and horror
   Ever since, though those first years with George were great.
He's lively. Here's one thing I'll always love him for:
   Driving up the driveway once, he asked how I would rate
His speech, and when I said, he drove into the door.

Colin Powell's March

My name is General Colin Powell.
I did object but never howled.
As a soldier, I'd grown residential,
But people called me presidential.
I was black and much respected,
So once they got their boy elected,
I was naturally selected
Secretary of our State.
I took notes and swallowed bait.

Resign! Don't say it!

Oh, I had concerns about this pack,
Yet, as a practiced bureaucrat,
I figured I could hold them back;
But these were giant rats on crack,
The boy some kind of Superbrat.
I might have quit, since they alarmed me,
But that's not why I joined the Army.
I thought I'd put the brakes on them;
Instead, I had my honor taken.

That's heartbreaking!

They turned me into cannon fodder.
A soldier gives and follows orders.
That's who he is, his definition.
They gave me lousy ammunition
With which to face the United Nations.
I worked like hell to edit it,
Wondering who'd credit it.
Still, I played tough. I'd eaten rations,

Good soldier that I was, old-fashioned,
Who'd eaten my fair share of shit
And grown to like the taste of it.
No one makes it through the ranks
Without smiling and saying thanks.

No thanks. No thanks.

The evidence I gave was fake,
And, looking back, it's hard to take
The truth of how I was abused,
A colored condom they had used.
They wrecked the Army and my name.
All I can do is bear my blame.

What a shame. What a shame.

A Beautiful Mind

My name is Barbara Bush. I have a lovely mind,
  Just beautiful. It's obvious that I don't jog
  Like Junior or his dad. Instead, I keep a log,
An annotated list of those who've been unkind
To me and mine. I often go there, in my mind,
  And blow them up like Junior used to do to frogs.
With my own mind, I wrote a book about our dog
Millie, a charming legacy we'll leave behind.

So when that awful woman had the gall to ask
  If once our military hit Iraq I'd find
Myself disturbed by images of body bags,
  I asked her back why I would waste my lovely mind—
Where I had gone, right then, to view, behind my mask,
  My rotten enemies laid out in one long line.

Vice

The family, who knew I was seasoned and wise,
   Invited me in to appraise the race,
And the Dummy decided I'd make a nice vice,
   An ambitionless man who would stay in his place.
      I'd talk straight through his face.

We managed to get the young man elected,
   With his brother in Florida, good work in Ohio,
And SCOTUS ensured the right guy was selected.
   We'd got by November, and then, me-oh-my-oh.
      Jiminy Christmas. Ho, ho.

We'd been lying in wait since they'd taken down Nixon
   For the chance to remake America great.
I'd get Rummy appointed; Don had been fixing
   For years for a fight, and he and the Dummy'd relate;
      They both could lie so straight.

I'd long thought we needed a second Pearl Harbor
   To bring this great nation, this slumbering giant, awake
To the dangers and also the chance for the marbles
   Worldwide. There were risks I'd be willing to take
      And laws that I would break.

One might say the Saudis had answered my prayer
   When they brought our birds down out of heaven
(One regrets, naturally, the loss of life there.),
   Creating the master disaster of grim nine eleven.
      I'd use what we'd been given.

One was right: A wounded nation was easily led.
    The Dems lined the Hill like birds on a shelf
And sang, seeing stars and stripes in their heads.
    Later, when someone objected to stealth,
        I said, "Go fuck yourself."

One shouldn't regard one's boss with derision,
    But while they had the boy flying about,
I went underground and issued decisions.
    The way he sat frozen with *My Pet Goat!*
        That man gets my vote.

His handlers corrected the imagery trouble
    By sending him out to the site with a bullhorn
And some tired guy he could hug on the rubble,
    And though it was nothing but PR porn,
        A hero he was born.

No problem invading Afghanistan
    Since bin Laden had built his bases there,
But the place is nothing but poppies and sand.
    Those ragheads had nothing that they could share,
        But you know who's next door.

One needed a rationale for Iraq,
    But a Quaker could see that Saddam was bad,
And the nuclear threat would sell the attack.
    Saddam had gone after the president's dad,
        And he'd stayed hopping mad.

Having learned what they needed for hotshot careers,
    We embedded and easily swayed the reporters.
Cutting off access makes everything clear,
    And owners and editors give them their orders.
        And so we crossed some borders.

Of course, one suffers along the way.
    One's lesbian daughter caused one disgrace,
And then when one's hunting pal got in the way,
    He said he was sorry but couldn't erase
        The fact I'd shot him in the face.

But globally speaking, one did rather well.
    The milquetoast Dems could never spoil
The way we had turned Iraq into hell,
    Where we'd have to stay, right next to the oil,
        And that was worth my toil.

So one pretty much got what one wanted. I'm pleased,
    Though there's more to be done. Nothing's final;
One has one's responsibilities:
    Iran. And Russia needs a reminder.
        And then, of course, there's China.

Misunderestimation Statement

You think my dad thinks Bill's a better man than me?
They fly around the world together. Did you see?
He's always just misunderestimated me.

Bill takes the floor so Poppy sleeps more comfortably.
They're both past presidents, but someday they'll be three.
You think my dad thinks Bill's a better man than me?

How not grateful would you guess a man could be?
I got the guy who tried to off him. Now he's free!
He's always just misunderestimated me.

I never gave him grandsons, but, gee criminy,
I doubled down on twins! You'd think that oughtta be . . .
You think my dad thinks Bill's a better man than me?

I knew when we bonked Baghdad, Dad would not agree
With that. But he's an oilman, for goodness . . . Shee.
He's always just misunderestimated me.

Or may- . . . You think he's boughten Bill and Hillary?
The man is smart. And look, hell's bells, he fathered me!
You think my dad thinks Bill's a better man than me?
He's always just misunderestimated me.

Laura's Lament

Were you aware that back in 1968
I volunteered for Democratic candidate
Eugene McCarthy? No? I had great scorn for greed,
And you could count on me in case you needed weed.
Then I met George, and, blam, that man came after me
With such intensity he altered my biography.
Just like that, of course, I turned Republican.
I'm stunned to think . . . the things that we won't do for men!
I don't know where he went when I was pregnant with the twins,
But I left literature around the house for him,
And he did change himself . . . as I had changed for him.
That was my victory, and we went on to win . . . and win . . .
Though I catch myself in tears sometimes because
I'm not . . . the *world* is not what I once thought it was.

Dr. Yes: Alberto Gonzales

Senator, it seems to me most curious
That you should ask again about the odious
Nickname Ashcroft pinned on me: "Dr. Yes."
I denied that invidious characterization yes-
Terday and say the same today. It's hideous
To suggest I was a yes-man, though dubious
Claims are often made, Sir, by the envious,
As you must know. But I was not obsequious
To this or any other president. Yes,
I did write memos some have called felonious
Or worse, but consider, Sir, the very *pièce*
De résistance of this administration, imperious
As you may think it is, has been to be victorious,
And that, you must agree, is not vainglorious.

The Nutcracker

Our extended family calls me Bar,
    Although my boys will joke that I'm The Nutcracker.
    I lost my first, blonde daughter, a disaster
That bent and tempered me into a crowbar.
My steel, my husband's oil took us far:
    I made First Lady (Some said, "More like Mother"),
    And now, with W, I'm mother to another.
I loved George so hard it left me scarred
When he spent decades with that other woman.
    To think of her today still stirs my gorge
And turns my veins all fumy-hot with venom.
    Dick Nixon liked me more than he liked George.
Dick called him squishy, said I was vindictive.
    No. I died . . . but then determined I would live.

Pop Gives a Talk

Now I know how Muskie must have felt,
As if somebody'd given you a belt
So that you saw a thousand points of light.
We really tried to bring that boy up right,
The best of nannies, but he kept going wrong.
His brother Jeb was who we'd counted on
For presidential timber, smart and smooth,
But dumb luck struck the one who was uncouth,
Who couldn't spell and liked to blow up frogs.
I warned him. I said, "Son, unleash the dogs,
And they may very well come back to bite you."
He'd gone John Wayne and had his own advisers.
  But Barbara carried, cradled him. We raised him,
  And it's hard to see how everybody hates him.

"It's Just a Goddamned Piece of Paper!"

If your sister had died, and you didn't,
  You didn't, you didn't know why,
And your parents went off and went golfing,
  And they never, they never said why,
And your granddaddy played with the Nazis
  And your dad with the CIA,
Then why should some damn Constitution
  Stand in a cheerleader's way?

If your mom was a meanie but funny
  And your daddy was always away,
If you never thought squat about money
  Or wondered if you'd have to pay,
And your granddaddy played with the Nazis
  And your dad with the CIA,
Then why should some damn Constitution
  Stand in a frat brother's way?

If you took a small firecracker
  And stuck it straight up a frog's butt
And then lit the fuse, what would happen?
  Some gory good fun, tell you what!
When your granddaddy played with the Nazis
  And your dad with the CIA,
Then why should some damn Constitution
  Stand in an oilman's way?

If your dad saved your ass from the service
  In far away warm Vietnam,
Then why should you ever feel nervous
  And, really, why give a damn?
When your granddaddy played with the Nazis

And your dad with the CIA,
You can piss on the damn Constitution.
  A pilot can fly away.

If you can't take a drink, and you want to,
  And you used to suck snow up your nose,
Your side is Lone Ranger and Tonto,
  And everyone else simply blows.
When your granddaddy played with the Nazis
  And your dad with the CIA,
Then why should some damn Constitution
  Stand in a team-owner's way?

If you're saved and, Jesus, Christ loves you,
  It's good 'cause you sit beside God;
You're sort of like his lieutenant,
  And he's, like, the Boss of the Mob.
When your granddaddy played with the Nazis
  And your dad with the CIA,
Then why should some damn Constitution
  Keep you from feeling okay?

If you never read well in the first place
  And the letters kept moving around,
Then words on an old piece of paper
  Are something to flush underground.
When your granddaddy played with the Nazis
  And your dad with the CIA,
Then why should some damn Constitution
  Stand in a governor's way?

If your opposition is chicken,
  You can stick the flag up their ass,
Stand back, and enjoy the explosion.

They won't even offer you sass.
When your granddaddy played with the Nazis
   And your dad with the CIA,
Then why should some damn Constitution
   Stand in a president's way?

If the people stay happy with NASCAR
   And shopping and football and beer,
The Constitution's T-paper
   And not a damn thing to fear.
When your granddaddy played with the Nazis
   And your dad with the CIA,
You just gotta goose 'em a little.
   They'll welcome a dictator here.

When your granddaddy played with the Nazis
   And your dad with the CIA,
Ain't any damn Constitution
   Gonna stand in a torturer's way.
You do what you want when you want to
   'Cause that's a Decider's way,
And you buy a big ranch you can run to
   In beautiful, warm Paraguay.

February Thaw

It's nice to see asphalt again,
The glitter of bottles and cans.
    After living through blizzards
    And snow to our gizzards,
It's nice to see asphalt again.

It's sweet just to stand on concrete.
After flailing around with your feet,
    After slipping and sliding
    And clumsy colliding,
It's sweet just to stand on concrete.

You can keep your tulips and such,
But show me some cigarette butts,
    Dog turds and newspapers,
    Dead candy-bar wrappers,
And keep your damn tulips and such.

Don't you love the aroma of mud?
Before the leaves burst from their buds,
    Before the trees bloom,
    We can sniff this perfume.
Don't you love the aroma of mud?

It warms both my heart and my thumbs
To stand in the glare of the sun.
    It's fun to be knowing
    Just now it's not snowing.
It warms both my heart and my thumbs.

Minnesota Clerihews

Also Known As

Robert Zimmerman, who stole the poet's name of Dylan,
Thought his home town, Hibbing, was some kind of villain,
Took to the road, held audiences riveted,
And eventually cut a record called *Highway 61 Revisited.*

A Prairie Home Wake-up Call

As a young radio announcer, Garrison Keillor
Used to be quite the glockenspieler;
One morning he played six times in a row
"Blueberry Hill" by Fats Domino.

Minnesota's Nobel Prize Winner

Harry Sinclair Lewis
Should never be confused with Meriwether Lewis,
Who was far more athletic, nor with Upton Sinclair,
Also a novelist but without the red hair.

The Pileated Woodpecker

Is black and jumbo, like a crow.
Whenever I spot one, I go, "Oh!"
Among the birds I like the best,
He has a shocking scarlet crest
And looks terrific in the snow.
He's got a lightning streak of white
From beak to neck and down his side.
There's white beneath his inky wings,
And when he flies, it's startling.
His call goes *whicker, whicker, whicker,*
Not unlike—though louder than—the smaller flicker.
You'll see him swoop from trunk to trunk
And hammer holes that who'd have thunk
A bird could make with head and bill,
But he's the one responsible.
He's after grubs, a heavy feeder,
Much like me, a big meat-eater.
He loves the fragrant northern forest,
And I do, too, of course,
So it's possible that we're related,
Me and the pileated.

The Sleepytalk Man

Once there was a man who took to talking in his sleep
As if his dreaming were a horse race he'd been hired to announce.
His wife gave him her elbow or pummeled him with pillows,
And this went on for years of nights, but still they stayed a couple.

> So much in love with them were they,
> So deep in love and there to stay.

One day she heard him mutter in his morning coffee cup
And whisper up his jacket sleeve before he pulled it on.
He spoke into his rubber boots. He mumbled in his scarf.
She shushed him when she hugged him, pleading, "Can't you please
    shut up?"

> But still they stayed in love with them,
> Both he with her and she with him.

He said, "This talking trouble has to be my parents' fault.
They hissed at us and hollered, 'You little creeps, keep quiet!'
I was good, but now, I guess, when I'm no longer small,
You hear what happens once a man comes off a talking diet."

> And still she loved him, yes, she did,
> And he her all the more.

Her understanding didn't help. He barked at the TV.
He seemed to be a radio. He shouted in his hat.
He hollered into culverts. He spoke out loud in church.
People called him crazy. She couldn't live with that.

> But still she stayed, in love with them,
> Her favorite half of whom was him.

One night when he was talking from the bottom of a dream,
She hummed a weird half-witted waltz that sounded like a hymn.
Next morning he was calm. She thought, If he's not roaring
All day long, what's wrong with sleepytalk? He could be snoring!

    So steep in love with them they stay,
    Still sleepy deep in love today.

The Thinker

Does a ring around the moon mean more than rain?
Such questions kept me up at night.
Does the soul exist outside the brain?
Does a ring around the moon mean more than rain
That finally falls to save the grain?
Is there any such thing as second sight?
Does a ring around the moon mean more than rain?
Such questions kept me up at night.

O'Gara's Bar & Grill (circa 1978)

The Northern Star Ceili Band
Fiddles for fun, for free. Jammed
On floppy folding chairs, crammed
Knee to knee, Jamie and Sam
Flay catgut while John
Beats bones on the taut bodhran.
Pat and Laura flourish flutes, and
Someone shouts, "Goddamn!"

The man who taught the kids these tunes
Grins and diddles his accordion.
This Celtic jazz fulfills a need
In Russian, German, Pole, and Swede.
Philip sips the pennywhistle,
And notes float free like thistledown.
Ross cups a hand around one ear
And calls a ballad from the air.

Jim comes in from the picket lines.
In the other room, the president lies,
Trapped in a little electric box.
Nick stomps and spins. The president talks.
Now Sheila's up. They reel and whirl,
Hips and hair. Her skirt unfurls.
A fiddle case wearing a loud decal
Declares that *Music Can Save the World!*

Nightnoise

Ducks talk quietly among the barren stalks,
Quarreling incessantly. Who should lead the flock?

Muskrat bloops below the surface of the stream.
Moon covers everything with light like cream.

Back in the forest, did a branch go screak?
Last of the mosquitoes wants to bite my cheek.

Mice like to rummage in the pots and pans.
Beaver whacks the water like a screen-door slam.

Starlight crackles in the cold night air.
Nothing makes a noise, and it isn't even there.

Jukebox Tunes from the Dirty Shame Saloon

Her Perfume Smelled Like Bug Dope and He Can't Forget
Evergreen Blues
Oh, for Nice
Meet Me in the Fish House and We'll Somehow Find the Room
Voices Sure Sound Louder over Water
The Peat Bog King of Koochiching
You Might Wear Moosehide Mukluks but You've Got an Ugly Truck
Blueberry Boogie
The Oil Can Rag
Ufda Mega, Mama, There's a Teardrop in My Eye
Where Have All the Crewcuts Gone?
You Must Be a Mosquito, Babe, 'Cause You Sure Love to Whine
The Trout Creel Reel
Phooey on You
Somewhere North of Nowhere, Everything Went South
Shotgun Schottische
Lake Superior's Wide and Blue and So, My Love, Are You
The Trouble with Linoleum
When I Think Back on Lutefisk and Lefse Warm and Dry
My Man's an Iron Miner but He's Not Made of Steel
Snowshoe Shuffle with a Boy Toy
The Cedar Swamp Stomp
When the Smelt Buckets Are Loaded, I'm Coming Home to You

How Big Are You?

When we're little, we are small,
Although we feel we're massive.
How big are you? Sooo big! Everybody laughs.

At ten, we streak around like comets,
Bits of ice and fire flying from our hair.
Try to stop me and I'll knock you down!

At twenty, we feel tall as mountains,
Casting shadows on the lowly plains.
You can almost touch the stars!

At thirty, we're big boulders,
And we rumble down the hillside.
Avalanche! Run! Run for your life!

At forty, boulders break.
How did that happen?
Sharp new edges, a vein of quartz exposed.

At fifty, we are pebbles on a stony shore,
Smooth as turtles, warming in the sun,
Touching other pebbles here and there.

At sixty, we are sand grains on a shining beach.
How small we seem, surrounded by so many
Our same size, but still we shimmer.

And then the tide takes everything we own.
We are dust motes, and we know it,
Some dancing in the light, some not.

v

What My Daughter, Who Is Always Reading, Said

When we had eaten lunch, a happy meeting,
The bookstore still a happiness ahead,
My daughter, who is always reading, said:
"The two of us are very much alike
'Cause you love books, and I love books, love you.
Hey, give us a smooch right here, book lover!
But even when you're having, like, you know,
A swell, terrific talk—with people that you love!—
(Tell me if this isn't true for you.)
A part of you is thinking (This is awful.
Hey, my fuckin' heart is bleeding!), but
All this time you're listening and talking,
Smiling, sure (It's real; it's not demeaning.),
You also think: 'Ya know, I *could* be reading.'"

A Cautionary Tale for Condition Cranks

Nicholas Basbanes tells the story
How, in a rare book room at Middlebury,
A librarian showed him a bag full of parts
Unlikely to quicken a collector's heart,
Even had the book been whole: Asa Gray's
Manual of the Botany of the Northern United States,
Commonly found in excellent shape,
Although it was published in 1848.
And this one had plainly been studied to pieces,
Which means the value radically decreases.
The tattered thing lay there like a roadkilled crow,
The flyleaf signed "H. D. Thoreau."

The Bone Yard

A serious Buddhist student in Tibet
Will often climb the mountain to the bone yard
Where, because that barren country's frozen hard,
Humans, when they die, are hacked to bits.
If talented, that's where you're sent to sit
And see how rats and vultures have devoured
Those who once were good with tools and words,
Many of them highly talented.

So I would urge young poets worth their salt
To find a bookstore dim with dust and grime
And sit each week among the dumb results
Of poets, often famous in their time,
Whose work somehow has turned unreadable.
They, too, believed in metaphor and rhyme.

Hunger

John Clare, the peasant poet, who was labeled
"Weak but willing," five feet tall, was barely able,
Because he had too much and more to do,
To keep his family fed while he kept writing, too.
He found odd jobs—thresher, gardener, cowherd—
Outside work he naturally preferred,
Transforming into verse what he observed,
Doing double time, unknown to those he served.

His poverty persisted once he published.
Fine paper was a dream, a great white wish.
One time he wrote on birch bark he had stripped.
The ink he brewed has turned some manuscript
Bizarre, its paper browning now, with age,
Where homemade words keep eating through the page.

J. F. Powers and the Fiction of Perfection

1.

The man had a face like an axe,
The head of a hawk. The eyes—
Were they gray, blue, green?—
The eyes had a look
You don't see much these days . . .
You felt you were being appraised
From a long way off. Not without
A glint of kindness. Or was it
Amusement?

2.

Post World War II, Jim Powers,
Conscientious Objector,
Met a drunken vet at a party
Who snatched a butcher knife off a table,
Pressed the point against a button
Of the pacifist's shirt and shouted, "You
Son of a bitch, friends of mine died!"
Pressing, pressing, harder, harder,
Hissing, "You sorry, sorry son of a bitch."
Powers said calmly, "My friend,
You did what you believed in,
And so did I." The knife withdrew.

3.

The most frightening Christian
I ever met. It was nothing he said.
It was there in his bearing, straight
As a knife. He and his wife
Lived on little or nothing,
Sustained by a garden,

Castoff clothes, an old station wagon
They seldom drove. He wore khaki
Pants with a matching shirt
Buttoned right up to the neck,
Self-appointed custodian
Of the basement of heaven,
Mindful of warnings:
"Go to now, ye rich men,
Weep and howl for your miseries
That shall come upon you."

4.

He wrote primarily
About priests, their situation
His obsession. Some were humble,
Even noble, most obnoxiously
Unctuous in public, while in private
They might snicker over sex,
Drink nothing but the best.
None soared so high or saw
With such X-ray vision
Our ironic position. In Powers' fiction,
The priest, in the privacy of his study,
Putts the white ball across the carpet
Into his clerical collar. He sees
How the ladies leave their lipstick
On the crucifix they kiss.

5.

Jim liked jazz and little jokes.
Invited once to a student dance—
Bright horns blared, the drummer
Shushed and brushed the snare—
Powers appeared in the same sport coat

He always wore, with a saxophone neckstrap
Instead of a tie, and told everyone:
"I can't stay long. The Duke
Wants me upstairs with the big band soon."

When his wife lay bedridden
With cancer, he stood before her
Each morning with pencil and pad
To take her order: "Eggs or kisses?"
"Sunnyside up," Betty said.

6.

His course description
For Advanced Fiction:
"No text. No tests. No classes.
10,000 words."

7.

The Great Reviser, he wrote
Rough drafts of his autograph.
The last time I saw him, he wondered
Whether he might slightly alter
A line by Browning for carving
In the granite of his wife's gravestone.
Ask, "Jim, how's the novel?"
And he liked to say, "I've got problems
Nobody can help me with."
How he relished that! The grand
Existential loneliness
Of a day at the office:

Hang up your coat, sit, write a few words,
And cross them out. Stand. Pace.
Gaze out the window. Try again.

And again. An apple for lunch. Then
Try again. Tune in the ball game. Snap
The radio off. Lie on your back
On the hard oak desk
And cross your arms,
Practice for the casket.
Snooze. Try again. Give up.
Go to Mass. Pray. Pray hard.

So the years passed.
It might take him all day to write one sentence.
If he published it, by God, he meant it.

The New Clerk at Barnes & Noble Recites for Me in Russian

Approaching the counter to pay for a scarlet notebook
That looks, to me, Russian, with gold filigree,
Confident I shall compose great Rachmaninoff,
Astounding Tchaikovsky concertos of poetry
In such an extravagant tablet, I seem to be hearing things:
Does the new brunette clerk have an accent? Indeed,
She does. *Do svidanya*, she does. *Perestroika*, she does.
She is middle-aged, slim, and intense. "I like your accent," I say.
"Are you Russian?" "Yes," she declares, "that I am."
The manager intercedes, introducing me with a flourish,
With my provincial title, hard-earned. "This is Barton Sutter,
Poet Laureate of Duluth." I flush with provincial pride.
"And this," the manager says, opening her hand to her clerk
And closing her eyes to recite, "is Irina Alexanderovna Miloserdova."
I am destroyed, completely eclipsed. Imagine: to have a name
Like a compound, complex sentence straight out of Dostoyevsky!
Who could mistreat, who could insult a woman with such a name?
For a name like that, we doff our fur caps and compete to surrender
    our seats in the sleigh.
For a name like that, the red carpet unrolls in the snow and we
    cover our hearts for the queen.

Still, I manage to blurt, "Is it true what they say about Russians
    and poetry?"
"Of course," smiles Irina Alexanderovna Miloserdova, "yes, it is
    true."
"Then would you, please," I request, my English already falling
    apart,
"To recite me a poem in your language?" "Of course," she agrees
And stiffens her already heart-stopping posture.

Out of her mouth like smoke comes the Slavic buzz
Of a poem that my poor American brain entertains
As the most profound nonsense: *the disheveled doves and zoot suits,*
The zoos on the brink, the cross country, double whiskeys, you think
Shoveled rinks and loved skates, pairs of pink strident hacksaws.
On she goes, this Irina, reciting with passion this poem that she knows,
And the roof of the store draws back, retracts, so we see
A samovar big as the Goodyear blimp floating above us,
The tea nearly ready, and I can smell chocolate besides.
Angels and archangels ascend and descend through the steam,
Singing hosannas, Anna Karenina throws herself on the tracks,
And packs of black wolves streak off through the snow
As Irina Alexanderovna Miloserdova recites Russian verse.

A rumba line of customers is pressing close behind me,
Leaning in to hear and grin, and *here* is the foreign language
Of poetry I longed for in the tiny tight-ass towns where I grew up,
Where all of us sat all over ourselves and strangled every operatic
    impulse,
Every heartsick desire, every extravagant longing for life.

Finally Irina concludes and gives credit with shining black eyes:
"Alexander Sergeyevich Pushkin." I want to leap over the counter
And kiss her full on the mouth, I want to bite both her cheeks,
I want to march her around on my shoulders, but this is America,
The Midwest, and I'm Swedish, besides, so I don't.

I reach for her hand and shake it and shake it
In my best Russian manner, inventing this as I go,
Shaking and shaking with, can I say, *vigor*?
Would that be okay? Shaking her very nice hand
With great *vigor*, yes? because I am happy, so good,
Thanks to you, very much, to make your acquaintance.

Driving through a Blizzard on New Year's Eve

Snowflakes blow by at unbelievable speed,
Like the thousand million specks of anger, guilt, regret,
The thousand million asterisks of lust and glad affection
That keep a couple coupled through the years,
And crunch beneath our spinning wheels
As we hurtle headlong down the swirling silver tunnel of our
     headlights.

Helpful Developments

Surely you've seen those sweet switcheroos
In couples who've made it to late middle age:
Boppa sits down with a doll in his lap
To take imaginary tea with the little neighbor girls;
Grandma goes out and buys herself a chainsaw.

Skin

I slip into bed and slide my hand
   Beneath your silky gown
To circle round and round your back,
   To feel you up and down.

That day we launched our new canoe
   The weather was a gift.
Pussy willows lined the banks,
   And we just let her drift.

Where'd summer go? What happened to
   Your cappuccino tan?
You lie here like white sand, my love,
   I'm smoothing with my hand.

The leaves are letting go the trees,
   And I'm the breath of wind
That finds the hidden, trembling pond
   The leaves are dropping in.

I'm skiing down a snow-soft slope
   And up another rise.
You stir beneath my hand and sigh,
   "That's awfully, awfully nice."

I've studied how to gentle you
   So you'll take me inside
And treat me to your satinslick
   Smooth electroglide.

Poem That Picks Up Where Neruda Left Off

I want to do to you
What spring does to the cherry tree,
What winter does to the Norway pine,
What autumn does to the maple tree.

I want to do to you
What the buck in rut does to the doe,
What the falcon does to the sharp-tailed grouse,
What the owl does to the meadow vole.

But I'd also like to be for you
The banjo twang in the bullfrog's throat,
The pollen dust on the windblown rose,
The where'd-she-go in the rabbit's coat.

And I would like to do for you
What summer does for the spotted fawn,
What showers do for the brook trout stream,
What water does for the long-necked swan.

For My Wife upon the Garage Roof

I'll say nothing of Donner or Blitzen,
Just the sixty-some-year-old vixen
   Whose rambunctious life I've now shared
   For several adventurous years,
Who has climbed upon the garage roof,
Whom I've handed up her triage stuff,
   Her long-handled loppers and saw,
   While holding the ladder in awe.
She is going right after those branches
(While I'm telling her, "Hon, don't take chances.")
   Of trees that are rubbing the shingles.

   I would rather be married than single,
And I've said there are those who will do this,
Professional men who'd conclude this
   For less than outrageous pay,
   But she's never cared much what I say.
She's a really formidable kisser,
And if she were dead, I would miss her,
   But the neighbors know well there's no stopping
   A project on which she's got hopping.
At the moment, she's hopped on the rooftop,
And it's looking to me like a long drop,
   Yet she's scooting on out to the edge,
   Which has got to produce quite a wedgie,
Then leaning way out with her clippers
To snap off offending tree tippers.
   The power lines failed to electrocute her,
   Which is good because, this way, she's cuter.

Now she's backing herself down the ladder,
With me feeling gladder and gladder
  And finding the moral at bottom:
  Rejoice in your wives while you've got 'em.

With You in Spain

Even though you'd gone to Spain,
The tulips came
Up like bright umbrellas yanked
Open by the wind
So that I grinned
And gave small thanks,
Even though you'd gone to Spain.

The lilacs held their soft
Sprays of lavender aloft
And made me glad,
Though I was sad
Because you'd gone to Spain.

My inner life was drab
Without you, but the flowering crab
Effervesced like pink
Champagne, a soft shellburst
Of fireworks
At which I blinked.
To think that such a color
Could occur
With you in Spain!

The apple by the garden
Bore big blooms like white gardenias,
Ghostly gatherings of moonlight
That glistered in the night,
But you missed your chance to see this
Because you'd gone to Spain.

The waves of blue forget-me-nots
That broke about the house were not
Meant for my eyes only,
So I absorbed their lowly
Beauty for us both, hoping you were homesick
For this side of the Atlantic
There in Spain.

Oh, I knew that you'd come back
And we'd glory in the crack
As you told stories
Both laughable and scary
And taught me Spanish names
For blossoms, trees, and rain.
My heart was hardly broken
Just because we hadn't spoken
Face-to-face for weeks.
That muscle's strong and sleek,
But it *was* severely strained
With you in Spain.

My nerves were somewhat numb,
But I could smell and see
The tiny blossoms of the plum
Invite the thirsty bees,
And I was plenty pleased
To watch them come,
Though they were dumb
About your whereabouts
In Spain.

I doubt
I can explain
The half of what you missed

By going off to Spain,
But if a tree blooms in the forest
And there's no one there to notice,
Is that lonesome festival of beauty real?
And how can unseen flowers hold appeal
For you in Spain?

I confess I walked the orchard,
Indulging in self-torture,
Envisioned us erased,
Another couple in our place,
Who seldom gave a thought
To those who'd planted what they'd bought.
The apples, plums, and cherries
Still remained and could be seen
In sunshine and in rain
But not by you and me.
Though the thought was little help,
I tried to tell myself
When we are dead and buried
It will only be
As if we've gone to Spain.

Let me try to make this plain.
Imagine you had seen
Apple petals drifting down
Like manna on the lawn,
But we were gone.

VII

The Reindeer Camps

1.

In reindeer camps,
We feed the fire first—
Vodka, tea, bits of meat.
We feed the fire spirit first;
It eats before we eat.
Otherwise, we'll have bad dreams.
We'll have bad dreams . . . or worse.
In reindeer camps,
We feed the fire first.

2.

In reindeer camps,
We like hot soup,
Those vegetables that keep,
And berries gathered fresh.
The reindeer come in close to camp
For milking in the dusk. We drink tea
And reindeer milk. We tote
Flour packed in gunny sacks
And sugar that we love so much
The white death makes our teeth turn black.
We net fish from waterways
And shoot sheep off the mountains,
But mostly in the reindeer camps,
We like eating reindeer.

3.

Of all the ways to hunt reindeer,
This one is the best:
Ride your favorite reindeer out
To where the wild reindeer are,

Dismount, let your reindeer wander
Out among the wild ones
But with a rope of braided hide
Tied around his antlers,
The other end around your wrist,
The rope unfurling off your arm.
Once your favorite finds a friend,
Slowly reel your reindeer in;
The wild one will come along
For you to shoot or knife.

4.

Two kinds of reindeer in this world:
Wild and half tame. Here is how
Reindeer came to live with us.
We hunted them, we followed them.
Dozens, hundreds, thousands
Flowed across the land like living lava.
Compared to them, we were so few
They did not panic at our camps.

One day one woman noticed
Females eating reindeer moss
Where she had pissed. They liked the salt.
So every day she urinated closer to her tent
Until, at last, they came, oh, yes,
Close enough to touch. She touched.
They let her pet, caress, and milk them.
So they came to live with us.
And wasn't that a crafty trade that woman made—
Milk and meat and bone and fur
For nothing more than urine?

5.

Come, let us bell the deer,
Just our leaders, gelded males.
I think that we have several here
To hang around their necks,
Fashioned from condensed milk cans
With spoons tied in to clang,
And then, held back for our best beasts,
These Buddhist temple bells
Of heavy Mongolian brass
Embossed with Tibetan prayers.

6.

We are quiet people;
It's what the land demands.
The animals don't shriek or scream;
They mumble to themselves.
No shouting from the mountaintops,
No singing on the trail.
The hawks cut circles, watching us;
The rocks are listening in.
Laments are best contained in tents,
Carousing kept in camp.
Sometimes the men will argue hot,
Forget themselves and fight.
A woman who encounters friends
She feared she'd lost for good,
Whose heart hurts, overpowered,
May sing out loud for hours.
But normally, we aim for calm,
Like timber wolf or swan.
When we arrive, we mosey up;
When we depart, we're gone.

7.

We walk and ride from camp to camp,
From spring to autumn slaughter,
From snow to rain and bugs to snow,
And seldom settle anywhere
For longer than a month or so.
To overgraze the grass and moss
Would be a grave mistake.

At dawn the deer disperse to feed
Through valley, mountain, wood.
We follow, keeping watch, with dogs,
And nudge them home at dusk.
We spook them just enough so that
They cluster, counterclockwise,
Turn and turn and tighten
In a breathing knot for night.

There may be berries in the woods,
A fragrant grove of larch,
A sweet supply of fish nearby;
That can't be helped. We move
To guard the grass and moss,
Which means to save the deer,
In other words, ourselves. We move,
And when we do, we don't look back.
We never say goodbye.
To say so sadly might imply
That someone's going to die.
But we are people of the deer,
And we come back by going on,
Appearing here next year.

8.

Lucky the man whose love loves him
And also loves the reindeer camps.
Women like the village now,
To work as teacher, nurse, or clerk,
To walk the street in long cloth coats,
To wear the shiny leather boots,
Pretending they're in Moscow.
The herders who come into town
Seem strange to them, can't talk
From listening closely to the wind,
To wolves, to grunting beasts whose hooves
Clatter over stone like clicking castanets.
Lucky the boy who finds a girl
Who loves the rippling willow leaves
Like minnows in the blue,
Who loves the shine of poplar leaves,
Their shifting in the sun,
Who loves the scent of larch needles,
Their perfume in the tent,
Who doesn't mind the rain and damp
But loves the ways to warm.
Lucky the man whose love loves him
And also loves the reindeer camps.

9.

Here's the horn
Of a mountain sheep,
Excellent for carving.
What should I make
Our little girl?
How about a little girl
Riding on a reindeer?

10.

In reindeer winter hunting camps,
Where we trap ermine, sable, wolf,
You have to wear a reindeer coat,
Keep reindeer blankets in the tent.
Nothing else will do. Only hollow
Reindeer hair will let you move and live
At 85 below. Always leave your coat outside
Because a tent can burn. Say you
Forget to feed the fire spirit;
Everything goes up.
You dive outside, your coat's inside,
Now what? Now what? You die.

11.

Taiga, taiga, world of white,
Home to sable, black as night,
What mere human mind or eye
Can take in your immensity?

In which valley, deep with snow,
Does the reindeer lichen show?
Will a white owl lead the way?
Broken voiced, can raven say?

Who might know in this domain?
Brown bear? Marten? Wolverine?
Since we've lost the shaman's drum,
Where will second sight come from?

Who will wear the antler crown,
Dance until he's fallen down,
Go inside to travel far,
Find out where best pastures are?

In this land of little sticks,
Who will heal the mad and sick,
Show the drumskin smeared with gore
After health has been restored?

Taiga, taiga, world gone white,
Home to sable, black as night,
What mere human mind or eye
Can penetrate your mystery?

12.
Transport planes have come and gone,
Russian agents come and gone,
Helicopters come and gone,
Communism come and gone,
Flocks of snow geese come and gone,
Poplar leaves gone gold and gone,
Reindeer herds go on and on.

13.
It's good to let us know the place
Where you would like to lie.
Tied high in a willow tree
Where sunshot water runs?
Relaxing in the spicy woods
Where moss grows soft as sponge?
Or skyhigh on a mountainside,
Your bones beneath a cairn?
If only you will let us know,
We'll try to take you there.

Or if you like, we'll burn big logs
To melt the permafrost
And dig as deep as you stood tall.

We'll shroud you in a reindeer robe,
A blanket, or birch bark,
But not one soul will sob aloud;
We don't want you to think
We miss you so we want to go
With you beyond the clouds.
We'll sacrifice your best reindeer
So you'll have him to ride
The skyscape where you're bound.
We'll eat his meat and hang his hide
To show he's gone with you,
And, likewise, we will kill those things
We leave as offerings
To help you on your way:
We'll smash the vodka, break your knife,
And snap the cigarettes
We scatter on your grave.

14.

How long have we herded reindeer?
Three thousand years.
How long have we hunted reindeer?
Ten thousand years.
How come, having died, then,
You're still surprised to see
Your favorite turn to gaze at you
Through frosty breath? As you
Approach, he walks away, then trots
As you begin to run,
And only as you sprint flat out
And sob for breath and flail,
You catch one antler at the root
Like someone clutching at
A sapling trunk while falling from a cliff.

You pull yourself at last
Upon his muscled, rippling back
And clutch both antlers now
Because he's running lightfoot free
And lifting off the ground,
So fast the tears flow from your eyes,
But still you see you're flying,
Flying toward the sun, the life
Beyond your life at last,
Finally begun.

Acknowledgments

I am grateful to the editors of the following magazines and anthologies in which some of these poems, or earlier versions of them, first appeared:

> *Great River Review*: "Poem That Picks Up Where Neruda Left Off";
> *Labor World*: "The Love Song of Karl C. Rove";
> *Lake Street Review*: "O'Gara's Bar & Grill (circa 1978)";
> *North Country Sampler*: "A Little Shiver";
> *Paterson Literary Review*: "My Father and the Trondheims," "The Plaster";
> *Ripsaw*: "The Minnesota Department of Transportation Plans to Straighten Out Highway 1," reprinted in *Wearhouse Catalog;*
> *South Dakota Review*: "An Afterlife After All," "Driving Through a Blizzard on New Year's Eve";
> *Talking River Review*: "Alakazam," "Dead Evergreens," "With You in Spain";
> *Trail Guide to the Northland Experience in Prints and Poetry*: "How to Say North," "Several Dozen Shades of Green".

Most of the poems in Section I are included in *Pine Creek Parish: A Verse Play with Music*, Book and Lyrics by Barton Sutter, Original Music and Arrangements by Marya Hart, originally produced and directed by Nadine Schmidt, Theatre Department, Southwest Minnesota State University, Marshall, Minnesota, in October, 2010.

All of the poems in Section III are included in *Bushed: A Poetical, Political, Partly Musical Tragicomedy in Two Acts*, Book and Lyrics by Barton Sutter, Original Music and Arrangements by Marya Hart, originally produced and directed by Brian Matuszak, Rubber Chicken Theater, Duluth, Minnesota, in October, 2008.

"The Reindeer Camps" was first published as a letterpress chapbook by Scott King's Red Dragonfly Press in April of 2008. This poem owes everything to *The Reindeer People* by Piers Vitebsky, including a few lines I simply lifted from Vitebsky's often poetic prose. The poem is intended as a tribute to his enchanting book and to the people and animals he studied.

"Hunger" is based on information in *John Clare: A Biography* by Jonathan Bate.

Thanks to Mary Pulford, whose very Northern remark in a parking lot inspired "February Thaw." And to Irina Alexanderovna Miloserdova Bogge for her magnificent recitation of a poem by Pushkin one memorable afternoon in a Duluth bookstore.

Thanks to my wife, Dorothea Diver, and to my stepdaughters, Lilo Kaiser and Bettina Stuecher, for their interest, patience, and support.

Thanks also to Anthony Bukoski, Carol Connolly, Philip Dacey, Milan Kovacovic, Howard Nelson, David Pichaske, and my brother Ross for critical comments and crucial encouragement.

Thanks to Peter Conners, Al Abonado, and all hands at BOA Editions for their thoughtful work on this collection.

And to Sophie's ghost, for all the walks in Chester Creek: *woof!*

Barton Sutter is a Fiscal Year 2011 recipient of a Fellowship from the Arrowhead Regional Arts Council with money from the Minnesota Arts and Cultural Heritage Fund as appropriated by the Minnesota State Legislature with money from the vote of the people of Minnesota on November 4, 2009, The McKnight Foundation, and an appropriation from the Minnesota State Legislature.

About the Author

Barton Sutter has earned the Minnesota Book Award for poetry with *The Book of Names: New and Selected Poems* (BOA), for fiction with *My Father's War and Other Stories*, and for creative nonfiction with *Cold Comfort: Life at the Top of the Map*. Among other honors, he has won a Jerome Foundation Travel & Study Grant (Sweden), a Loft-McKnight Award, and the Bassine Citation from the Academy of American Poets. In 2006, he was named the first Poet Laureate of Duluth. He has written for public radio, and he often performs as one half of The Sutter Brothers, a poetry-and-music duo. His collaborations with composer Marya Hart—*Bushed: A Poetical, Political, Partly Musical Tragicomedy in Two Acts* and *Pine Creek Parish: A Verse Play with Music*—have won standing ovations. Barton Sutter lives in Duluth, on a hillside overlooking Lake Superior, with his wife, Dorothea Diver.

BOA Editions, Ltd. American Poets Continuum Series

COLOPHON

The Reindeer Camps and Other Poems by Barton Sutter
is set in Centaur MT, a digitalized version of the font
designed for Monotype by Bruce Rogers in 1928. The italic,
based on drawings by Frederic Warde, is an interpretation
of the work of the sixteenth-century printer and calligrapher
Ludovico degli Arrighi, after whom it is named.

The publication of this book is made possible, in part, by the
special support of the following individuals:

Anonymous
Anne Germanacos
Suzanne Gouvernet
Robin, Hollon & Casey Hursh, *in memory of Peter Hursh*
X. J. & Dorothy M. Kennedy
Jack & Gail Langerak
Katherine Lederer
Peter & Phyllis Makuck
Boo Poulin
Deborah Ronnen & Sherm Levey
Steven O. Russell & Phyllis Rifkin Russell
Rob Tortorella
Ellen & David Wallack
Glenn & Helen William

❖